Play Wild!

PLAY WILD
Series

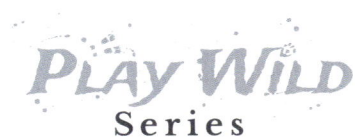

WHERE I FLY

A Hockey Story

Written & Illustrated By

K. M. ALLEN

Kat Allen

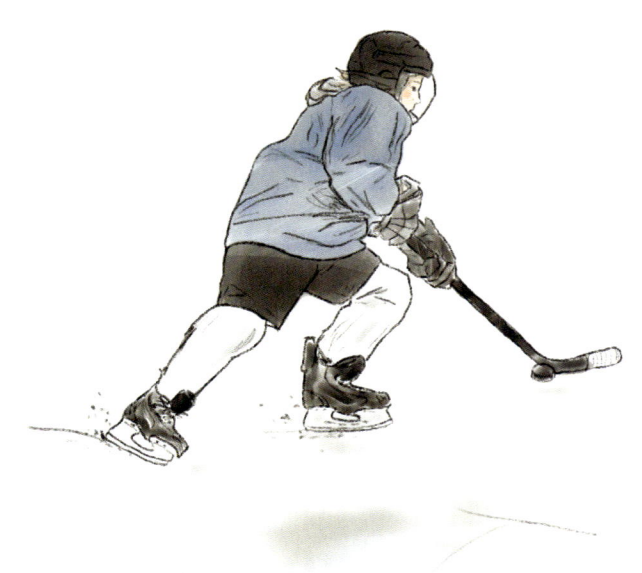

For Andy, Finn, and Max;
and for hockey players everywhere
under the stars.

With love & thanks to Aurora

Sweaters, mitts, sticks, skates . . .

Our footprints echo—we reach the lake.

Swish, swish—stride, glide . . .

The stars watch keenly as we fly.

Crisp air—*whissp, shhirrr*....

Giants awaken, shadows stir.

Whoosh, tumble, plop–slide!

The boards are snow drifts miles wide.

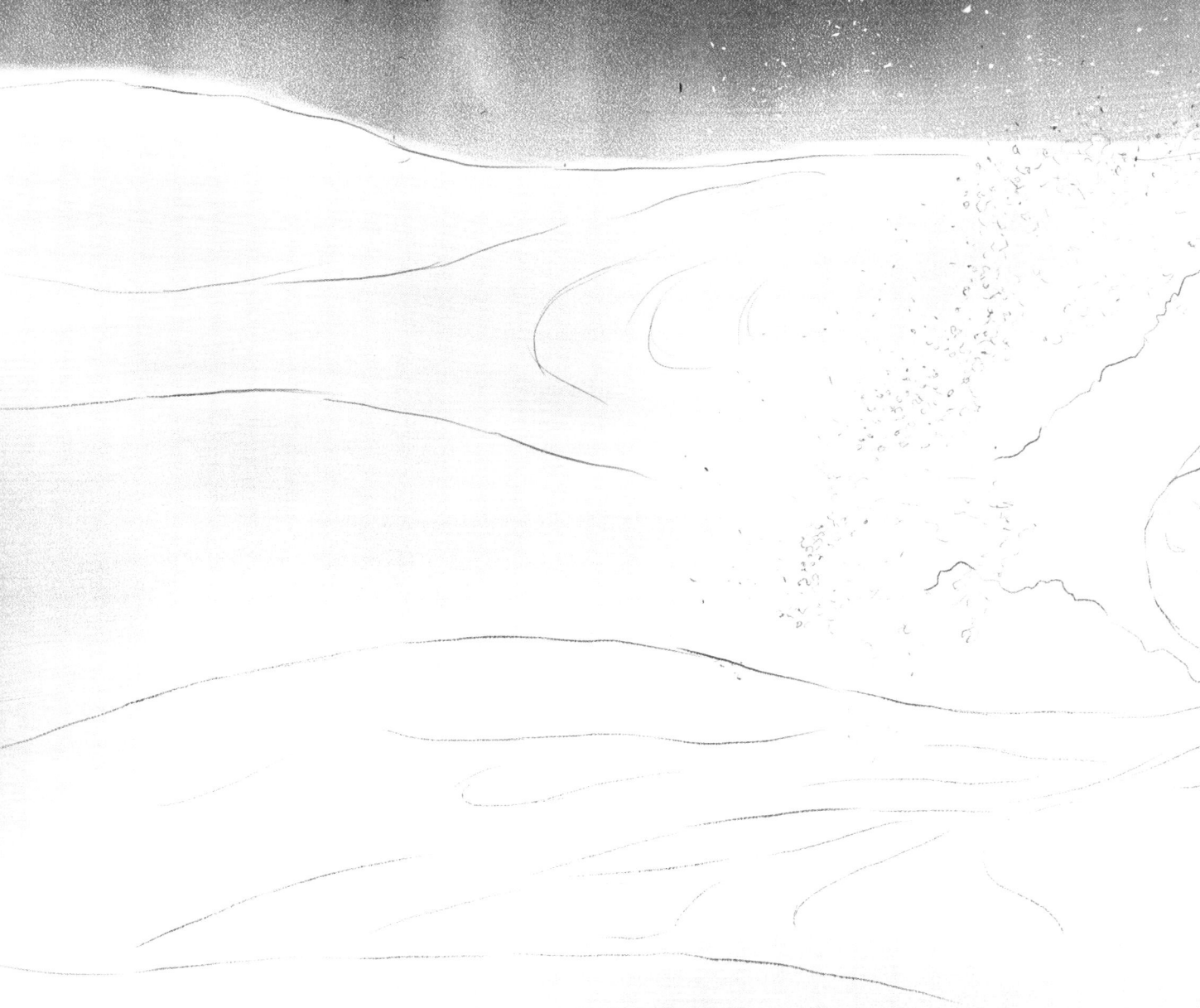

Blinking brightly all around—

Our forest fans don't make a sound.

Cloudy breath; our spotlights glow.

Shiny glaciers, spiraling snow.

Skate, *scrum*, rush, defend . . .

There's no beginning and no end.

Forward flying, *deke*—break free!

Even Dad can't catch me!

Against the wind—skate, flow, SOAR!

Beyond the trees, I hear the crowd roar.

Heel to heel, stick to stick–

Flying F A S T E R–watch my trick!

Snow, ice, stars, sky . . .

This is where I was born to fly.

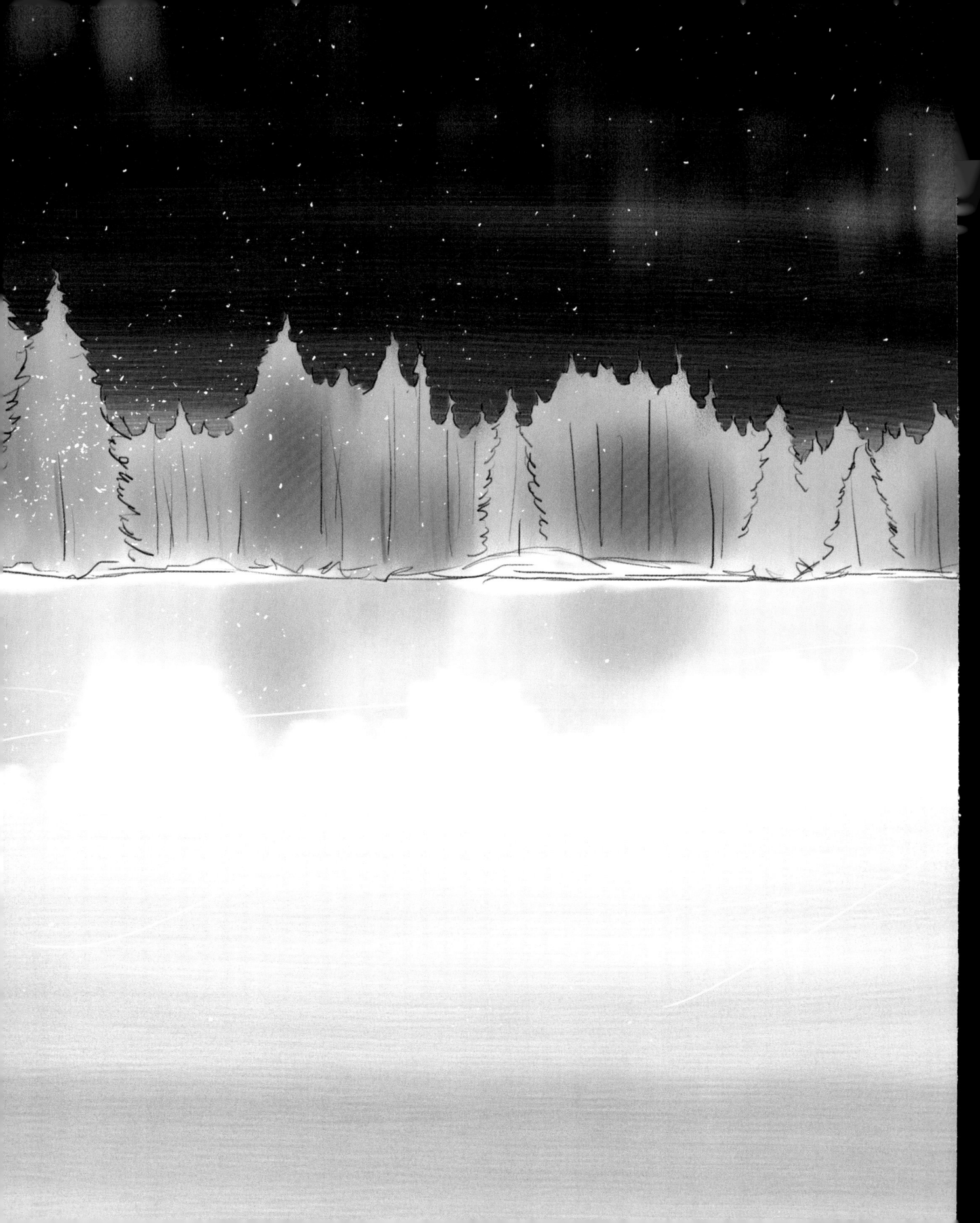

WINTER ANIMALS

Where I Fly takes place in a forest in northeastern Minnesota. Many animals live there! Some animals hibernate during the winter, but many animals stay active. *Can you spot these animals hiding throughout the pages of this book?*

White-tailed Deer are tan-colored mammals with white on their chests and tails! They live in wooded areas and eat plants. Male deer grow white antlers, and baby deer, or fawns, are covered with little white spots.

Moose are the tallest mammals in North America! They have thick brown fur and long legs. Usually found living near a lake or pond, moose live in forested areas as they love to eat twigs and other "woody" plants.

Gray Wolves are sometimes called timber wolves. They live in "packs"! Wolves can survive anywhere there is prey for them to hunt, as they are very versatile, intelligent carnivores with thick gray, white, brown or black fur.

Coyotes are very similar to wolves, but smaller. They love to talk to the others in their pack! Coyotes make all sorts of noises—howls, growls, yips, and barks—which can usually be heard if you're outside at night.

Snowshoe Hares are brown in the summer and their soft fur changes white in the winter! Fluffy, big feet help them run on top of deep snow! They make their burrows in forests where there are plenty of plants to eat.

Raccoons like to stay up all night! These clever creatures are known for raiding food from others, and the streaked, black fur around their eyes and tails make them look like mischievous little bandits!

Boreal Owls are small and like to hide—they are rarely seen by people! Their favorite foods are rodents, and they mostly like to hunt at night. White spots on their brown feathers make great camouflage in wooded areas.

Snowy Owls make their nests in far north, arctic regions, but they travel all around the world! They are beautiful, white birds with the perfect camouflage for snowy habitats, where they like to hunt small mammals.

Bobcats are light brown and gray wildcats with short "bob" tails and black tips on their ears. Catching their prey with their sharp claws and teeth, they also have amazing eyesight for hunting. This "kitten" will live with her mom for one year before venturing off on her own.

Do wild animals live in your backyard?

Share your drawings and photos of wildlife with us! *#PlayWildLife*

Go outside & *Play Wild!*

HOCKEY IS FUN!

Do you like to play hockey? Whether you're practicing on your own or rounding up a group of friends, hockey is a fun winter sport that can be played your whole life! Below are some "hockey words" that are used in this story:

Sweater / Mitts
Hockey jersey and hockey gloves worn over pads and hands for protection

Deke / Dangle
Crafty stickhandling used to move the puck around another player

Snap / Snipe
Shooting the puck with quick motion and precision to score a goal

Boards
The walls that surround the ice and designate the area of play

Scrum
A clash between two opposing players to gain control of or defend the puck

Pipes
The bars that hold up the hockey net; a puck "between the pipes" is a goal!

Have you ever played hockey outside?

Share your drawings and photos of outdoor hockey with us! *#PlayWildLife*

THE SKY AT NIGHT

Do you like to look at the stars? A galaxy is an enormous group of stars. Our sun is just one of billions of stars in our galaxy–the Milky Way! The Milky Way is a spiral galaxy, which means its shape is similar to a whirlpool. From Earth, the Milky Way looks like a curved cluster of stars across the sky.

A spiral galaxy

Auroras

Have you ever seen an Aurora? Auroras, or polar lights, are made up of tiny particles called electrons. They come from space in solar wind (wind from the sun) and go toward the Earth's magnetic poles. There, they get mixed up in Earth's atmosphere, and the sky glows bright *green, purple, pink, or blue* colors!

What is light pollution and how does it affect the sky at night? Too much unnatural light at night is called light pollution. This type of pollution wastes energy and causes the night sky to become dim and gray, not dark and clear–making it difficult to see and study space from Earth. Nocturnal animals, birds, and other creatures that migrate are also affected by light pollution. Too much light pollution will make our dark skies disappear.

Natural, dark night sky

What can you do to help stop light pollution? By turning off unnecessary lights and by using exterior lights that point downward, we can limit light pollution and discover more wonders in the natural night sky!

Night sky near a city with light pollution

WINTER CONSTELLATIONS

Have you ever picked out a picture in the stars?

Constellations are groups of stars. Each group is different and seems to make a pattern or shape in the night sky! Throughout history, people have named each constellation after the creature, shape, or mythological being that the stars resemble.

*If you live in the Northern Hemisphere, this "Sky Map" shows the **constellations** that can be seen in the winter!*

***Circumpolar Constellations** are close to the North Pole and can be seen all year round! Use this map to help find them (in blue), and in the night sky!*

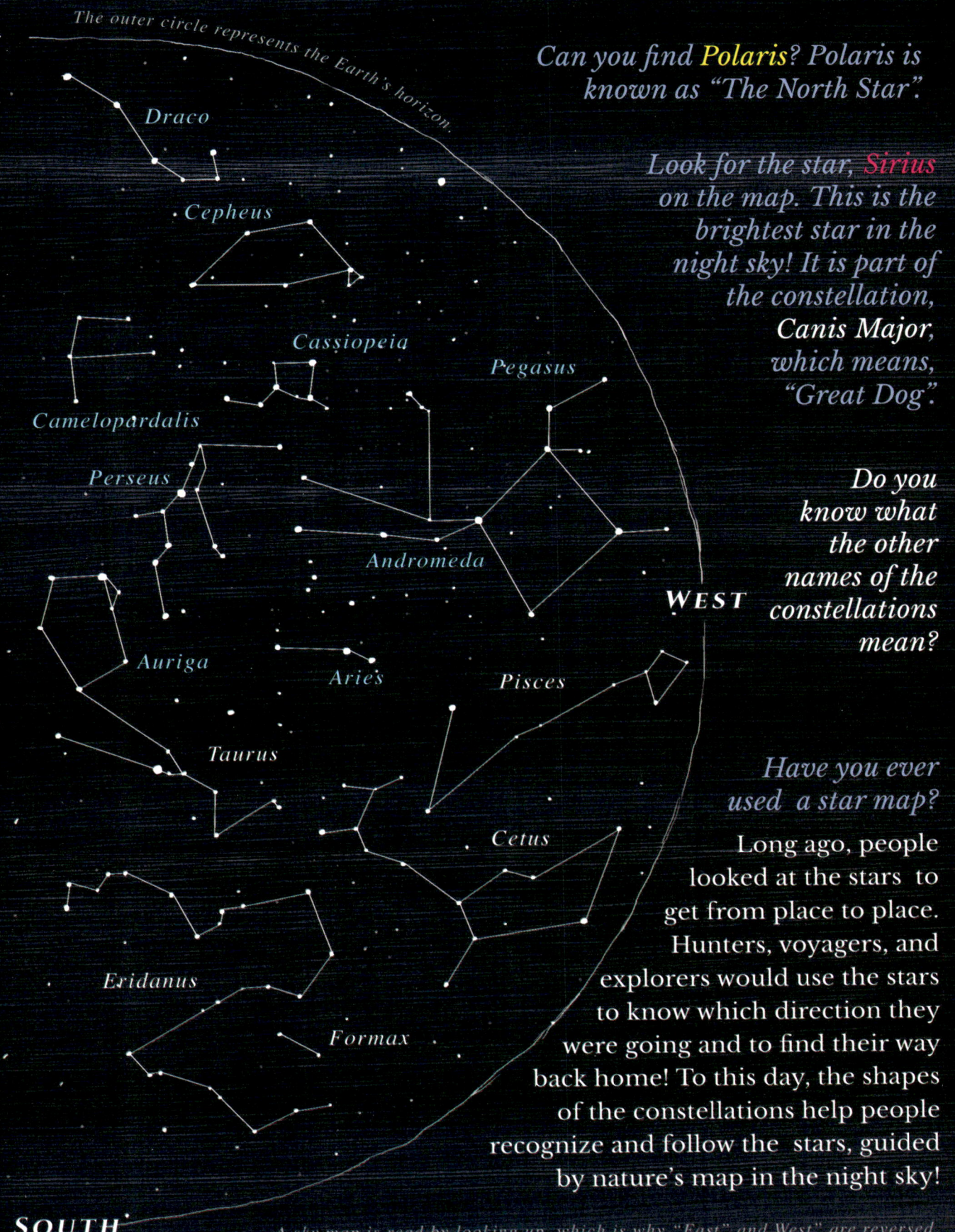

Where I Fly: A Hockey Story
Copyright © K. M. Allen

Published September 2018 by
Curious Cat Books
5 N. Central Ave.
Ely, MN 55731
1-800-909-9698
www.curiouscatbooks.com

ISBN 978-0-9904014-2-1 softcover
ISBN 978-0-9904014-3-8 hardcover
Library of Congress Control Number: 2018943367

All rights reserved. No part of this book shall be reproduced in whole or in part, in any form or by any means, electronic or otherwise, including photocopying, recording, or by any information storage or by retrieval system now known, or hereafter invented, without permission from the publisher.

Printed in the USA.